A sibling's uplifting introduction to Down's syndrome

written by big sister Mia, aged 9
with help from her Mum Hayley

Introduction

Hayley is married to Bob and they have 2 daughters, Mia and Natalia. Hayley is a writer and speaker, gently changing perceptions of Down's syndrome from within hearts with her words and images.

When their youngest was born with Down's syndrome, or Trisomy 21, they searched for a positive book that would help 2 year old Mia understand why her baby sister needed to spend some time in hospital.

They wanted to explain why the adults around her were worried and how she could get involved and help welcome the new baby into the family, sometimes giving her a little extra help and support.

Several years down the line and Mia has written such a book for other new siblings and family members, telling them how Natalia is a fun, but sometimes annoying sibling like any other!

It is a first introduction to Down's syndrome, accompanied by the family's beautiful photographs.

2

When Natalia was born she didn't come home from hospital straight away because she wasn't very well. Her heart needed some special care.

I was disappointed because I wanted my new sister with me.

The doctors and nurses looked after her really well, and I was allowed to go and visit her there when my cold had gone.

Mummy and Daddy were worried about Natalia and they sometimes cried.

Mummy and Daddy explained that Natalia has Down's syndrome. She has an extra chromosome in every building brick of her body, which I think looks like a jelly bean. It is just a part of who she is, like we both have brown eyes.

Lots of people say she looks like me when I was a baby, but I think she looks like Mummy and I look like Daddy.

She might always be a bit smaller than me and need extra help to learn to do things in her own way.

We all need extra help sometimes. I find it hard to tie my shoelaces on my walking boots by myself, and Mummy thinks of fun ways of helping me learn my times tables too.

7

When I visited Natalia in the Special Care Baby Unit I thought she was really beautiful.

When the nurses let me hold her she would try to open her eyes and look up at me.

I think she remembered my voice from the time when she was in Mummy's tummy, before she was born.

Natalia soon came home and got stronger.

I really liked spending time with her and I enjoyed being the big sister in charge!

I helped Mummy to look after her because babies are a lot of work!

When Natalia was 2 years old she went back to a special children's hospital to have a small hole in her heart fixed. It was a short operation and she was better very quickly.

I spent the day nearby with Grandma and we went to a science museum. I wished Natalia could come with us.

As soon as she woke up we went to visit her to give her love and gentle hugs and kisses and a present we had bought her.

I remember she blew a raspberry at the doctor who checked her that afternoon.

My little sister is so very funny!

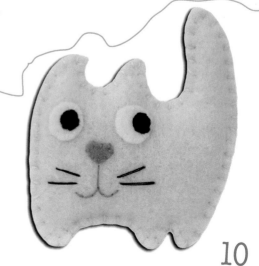

11

Sometimes Natalia had extra exercises to do, like:

Speech Therapy to help her talk. I learnt to use Makaton signing to help Natalia talk to me.

Physiotherapy to help her crawl and walk. Now she can swim and ride her tricycle.

Occupational Therapy to help her hold a pencil or spoon or fork.

Before she started school a lady came to our house to do Portage with us. This was lots of fun games and exercises we could play together with Mummy.

But mostly we just have fun together!

Dressing up...

Swimming and horseriding...

15

16

Going to school

17

learning lots
of new things

and going
on holiday

21

I like it when Natalia takes photos of me.

I like it when she kisses my sore knee better.

I like it when she pulls funny faces.

I like it when we read each other stories.

I like it when we dance in the kitchen.

I like it when she hides in my bed.

I like it when we play with our dog Pippin.

But sometimes she is really annoying, when she jumps on me or copies everything I say and do!

So I wrote her this poem:

To Natty
I love you so much
and you are the best sister in the world
and so precious to me.

You are so important to me
and if you weren't in this world
my life wouldn't be the same
and that wouldn't be fun.

So, I love you very very
much and you mean
everything to me..

Lots and Lots
of love from
Mia c

If you would like more information on Down's syndrome you can contact one of these organisation who have supported and advised us.

 British Institute of Learning Disabilities
www.bild.org.uk
0121 415 6960

 Down's Syndrome Association
www.downs-syndrome.org.uk
0333 1212 300

 Down's Syndrome Scotland
www.dsscotland.org.uk
0131 313 4225

 The Makaton Charity
www.makaton.org
01276 606760

 Mencap
www.mencap.org.uk
0808 808 1111

 Sibs
www.sibs.org.uk
info@sibs.org.uk
01535 645453

 National Portage Association
www.portage.org.uk
0121 244 1807

Scope
www.scope.org.uk
0808 800 3333

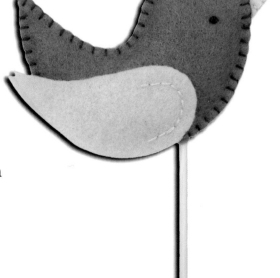

"With thanks to Sarah and Mark for their dedication and vision."

27

"There is something magical about becoming a big sister. A BIG sister! Suddenly you have a little partner in play and the occasional crime. As an adult I can see how our relationship has been a ribbon woven through my life and it's choices. Not because he told me who to become but because he helped me to know who I truly am."

Elizabeth Corcoran
Down Syndrome Research Foundation UK

www.DownsSideUp.com

Follow our journey on the award-winning blog www.DownsSideUp.com

©DownsSideUp2014 £5.99

ISBN 978-0-9929251-0-9

9 780099 292510
10599 >